The poems in *Raft of Flame* address inheritance haunted by colonial violence and genocide. The ghosts in the archives speak inside the poems, addressing heritage next to loss. "I don't see my face, owl says before soaring, / as the future is born of slave and colonizer / on the ledge of the window." Here we have the mysteries of mixed culture through the art made by the artists of the ancient Americas and Spain. Here a speaker asks, "I'm here to see where / I come from to stop the din of not knowing." The poems time-travel across regions, cultures, and centuries. Alvarez frets history, speaks to historical image-making, religion, and art. The poems invent new perspectives, speak in masks, present cinematic panoplies, are many-tongued, always clear-eyed. Richly they assemble, speak to story with mythic address as they sing and range. These poems are fire.

—Hoa Nguyen, author of *Violet Energy Ingots*
and Judge of Omnidawn's Lake Merritt Prize

A blazing vessel of insight carries us through the lush, devastated world of Desirée Alvarez's *Raft of Flame*. This book is propelled by questions—urgent questions that camouflage as ordinary ("And what time was dinner?" "How would a family look?"), and those that immediately chill: "Tell me why someone must always be sacrificed for the future to be assured?" Throughout, there is a dialectical heartbeat of desire and refusal. The gorgeous series of poems with "cante" in their titles weave Spanish with English. Alvarez knows and sings how both lineage and etymology carry relationships tender as well as coerced. These poems revel in and expose our sonic becomings: "Worship of ships now. Warship." And though the book is populated by other artists (Velázquez, Kahlo, Goya), it is Alvarez, here, who expertly wields both brush and pen.

—Stefania Heim, author of *HOUR BOOK*

Aboard this multilingual poetic vessel, Desirée Alvarez crosses the thresholds of time and space to enter ancient America and its conquest. On this journey, she examines the violent relations between the colonizer and the colonized, as well as her own entangled Latina, Spanish, and European heritages. A visual, eckphrastic impulse indelibly colors this collection, while a fertile lyricism echoes in its cante, its singing. In the end, *Raft of Flame* carries us to the place where we can look—entranced—into historical and genealogical "depths that cannot be uttered."

—Cra   *Threshold*

RAFT OF FLAME

Also by Desirée Alvarez

Devil's Paintbrush, Bauhan Publishing, 2016

RAFT OF FLAME

DESIRÉE ALVAREZ

OMNIDAWN PUBLISHING
OAKLAND, CALIFORNA
2020

Cover art:
Peacable Kingdom by Desirée Alvarez,
2007, ink on fabric, installation detail. www.desireealvarez.com.

Cover typeface: Kabel LT Std
Interior typeface: Kabel LT Std, Adobe Garmond Pro, and Cronos Pro

Cover & interior design by Trisha Peck

Printed in the United States
by Books International, Dulles, Virginia
On 55# Glatfelter B19 Antique
Acid Free Archival Quality Recycled Paper

Library of Congress Cataloging-in-Publication Data

Names: Alvarez, Desirée, author.
Title: Raft of flame / Desirée Alvarez.
Description: 1st. | Oakland, California : Omnidawn Publishing, 2020.
Identifiers: LCCN 2019048427 | ISBN 9781632430816 (trade paperback)
Subjects: LCGFT: Poetry.
Classification: LCC PS3601.L877 R34 2020 | DDC 811/.6--dc23
LC record available at https://lccn.loc.gov/2019048427

Published by Omnidawn Publishing, Oakland, California
www.omnidawn.com (510) 237-5472 (800) 792-4957
11 10 9 8 7 6 5 4 3 2 1
ISBN: 978-1-63243-081-6

for Michel

& in memory of my parents,
Augusta and Ramón

CONTENTS

VIOLET

AZURE

PORTRAIT OF A SPANISH MEXICAN MAID

Knock, knock, Velázquez. Can I come in?
I'm standing behind the man at the door. On the threshold
wearing my mantilla and cotton peasant dress.
Will you put me in the painting with the rest?
I'd like to warm my skeleton hands
in the heat of *Las Meninas.*
It's so brown in here I might be in a desert
or a forest. Or be Mexico.
I might finish the canvas for you,
show you what we gave up,
how we filled the sacrificial bowl
with blood and with vision, with giving and with taking.
I was thinking jaguar, I was washing paws.
The spots do not come out from a garment of eyes.

SMALL MODEL OF MEXICAN RUIN

All the sculptures, I would see with their eyes.
Across the centuries give me fox eyes,
iguana eyes, tortoise eyes. Eyes of eagle,
panther, jaguar, beetle. To be animal, to notice
the air shift at master's approach. To smell
the boar slaughtered in rain. To know who
were the Indians before the Spanish came.
Being of both sides, being of color.
Passing skeleton, fragile building of woman.

DIARY OF THE GHOST OF A MESTIZA

Written in the sorcerer's house *mis palabras*

are a mutilated palace
                    spread across a lake.

Elliptical pyramid. Oval. Oral.

My words are *manzanilla* crying
tea, storming the road yellow.

Mis palabras are heavy coated *coatis* trundling home to the jungle.

My words are great ant hills scarring the limbs of mangroves,
                    my words stalk black hummocks.

I sleep by the yucca so my words can taste licorice all night.

Mis palabras are mistletoe tangling *chechen* trees,
                    they fill the wood collector's bicycle cart.

Mis palabras are electrified seashells torching the dirt path
to the village smelling of dinner fire.

They are crisp leaves of poison underfoot.

My words are plants
blooming only on moonless nights. They say

let the land stay
        and the ruin stay ruined.

Let the vines come
and reptiles make their slow way across the dry earth.

Let great birds of hallucination return, and jaguars

take back the forest.

Let us, the ruthlessly
human, retreat.

TRADING POST

Swap an Aztec maiden for a cask of mezcal
or a swine for a boy. For compass follow the ship ahead
scanning the water for slaves fed to the sea.
Night divides between star and snake

to feed the sun its blood on the hill.
Clay pipe music sails white parakeets through the jungle.
The god of wind blows away his own lower face.
Corn, sleep tight in your green crib

while the warrior kills the rabbit, the deer, the moon.
What is family? A big conch shell carved of stone.
For sacrifice what will I use in place of my heart?
There's sap for my heart in the cottonwood tree,

make an exchange. The men will want to take it
in their hands. Give them the tree's heart instead.
Put it in a bowl and carry the bundle of flame,
corazón, carry it to the horizon.

UN TINTERO, INKWELL

Anger is the other person inside
    mi garganta, my throat.

      The mouth's mouth is the deepest.

Rage is the homeless boy fallen down a well.

Shout down and he will echo back.
        La lengua, tongue.

How long have you been down there?

        Subterráneo, underground.

The letters of Cortés are difficult to read,
      on each page a horse dies.

The lord of the city lives homeless in a canoe.
Hundreds of natives are speared.

      Another town is burned alive
      with all its caged creatures.

On each page the people appear to walk
          over their dead.

La tierra abonada, the earth fertilized,
spreads a cloth whose pattern repeats.

        On each page the future arrives
on a raft woven of snakes.

      Over and over, the design obliterates.

Never does he say *this was their home we took.*

CANTE DULCE

The god of dust must be
human touching everything
with his nearly invisible,
relentlessly soft coat.
Covering us with forget.

POEM ABOUT HOW TO HAVE A RELATIONSHIP WITH CIVILIZATION

First harvest the enemy,
then seduce the rain gods.

Poem that blows itself up then prays.
Poem insisting her dead body is still warm.

Massacre, masks, *máscara*.
Shield of color undercover of my skin.

GLINDA: Are you a black *bruja* or a white *bruja*?

ME AS DOROTHY: I was just looking for a home
and a new pair of shoes.

We carry a model of the world inside us.

To each her own version.

What words in Spanish do I most want to learn?
Guerras floridas, flower wars.

Now here's the pretty phrase
in *Nahuatl: xochiyaóyotl.*

Blood spurts from the neck
offering a red bouquet to sky's torch.

Moonlight killed for war,
fathom your last pregnant fire.

CALL & RESPONSE
BETWEEN COLONIZER & COLONIZED

Call the medicine man, call the fool, call the owl—
Tecolote, tecolote, tecolote.

I've held the bird so long it can no longer cry.
Lean is my nest and colorless.

Can you see your face?
Always a god behind the mask.

Savage layers, intestinal idols.
Depths that cannot be uttered.

Was there already a war before the soldiers arrived?
The shield moves first with feathers, then with snakes.

Are you born slave or tyrant?
I am vanishing on the threshold.

And did they change your language?
Look—how odd the word, a pair of eyes

and a harsh sound. Interruption—
Trance first, then entrance.

CANTE WITHOUT BORDERS

All roads cry after war.
I sing Spanish songs not knowing
how to pronounce the words
while the lavender moon guts
the highway with her audacious harvest
and the metalsmith hammers a bouquet
of steel roses for his mother.

COLOR COLORADO

Colorado, the word means red, named by early Spanish
explorers. Shepherds in the high Andes incant nineteen
steps between white and black. Did you feel different,
did they make you feel different? Myself, I did it, I made myself
feel so. Were you hidden, was your skin light enough, dark
enough, golden enough? Soft, it was soft, and I blended in,
I tried not to be noticed. Did you feel beautiful? No, never,
only once late at night alone in the bathroom. And why
did you look that way, where were you from, who were
your people? I did not know, I was not told.

CURIOSITY HAS MORE SYLLABLES THAN CONQUER

In the jungle when it's been raining for days I imagine
sunset as a red steak on a dish.

Every six or seven years he would visit to see how I was growing.
My braids all kinds of autumn colors. I am sure they loved

each other. Trees sending sugar collected from sun down
to roots for winter. And how mother wore her hair.

And what time was dinner? Underneath myth is the layer where
birds fly at you. No one is accountable. Drama without gods.

Drama with only weather and blood.
Pain forgotten but the drawings of parents recollected.

Even passion has a strategy.
History, let me in.

Here is the path the snake took, shedding skins along the way.
I'm collecting them to make a shroud.

AFTERWORD

Chile, chocolate, coyote, guacamole, mezcal, peyote,
tomato, ocelot, tequila—the words survive months of siege,
240,000 dead in Tenochtitlán. The Place of Herons,
a place of whiteness, did not survive. Duende, a tiny face
in a calla lily, survived. A bowl decorated with scorpion
and pelican survived. Clay faces full of shadow. Sculptors
who understood light, how it addresses the afterlife,
expecting a great dark to fall.

DEAR CONQUISTADOR,
WE ALREADY INVENTED THE WHEEL

The wheel beside me is a clay toy.
We sit together underground wrapped in skulls.
Mostly what I sense are bits of shell
still reeking of the brine of home.
I was made of clay too, by hands that believed
strongly. I can still feel their warmth
shaping my face and skin, the urn of me,
yearning Tlaloc of the wind, of the painted rain,
baked in sunlight. Who is to say I am not a god
all these years below earth? Surely not the ones
who came by boat and made us graven goods.
We knew all about velocity and we rejected it.

INDIGO, INDIGOING, INDIGONE

1519.   The artist of the tempest is dead.

Leonardo leaves behind his drawings   of whirlpools,
        tanks, flying machines,

                            inky details of empire building,

while Magellan sails the globe and Cortés lands in Veracruz.

In his second letter to Charles V,
Cortés tells his king he sees as many hues
for painters in the Mexican markets as in Spain.

Vendors selling twelve shades of dyed fur,

                            seventeen colors of woven jaguar
motif. Indigo plant, cochineal,
        the purple dye of sea mollusks.

        Harvest of the living by the living.

A hurricane is coming.

                    Gone—the earth's wild scale and man's.

All is now specific and small
                    as the eight-inch water lily spirit

    with an azure bird riding its head.

CARMINE

NOCHE TRISTE

Worship of ships now. Warship.

You are somewhere different, travellers.

Roast maize fills the air.

Tomorrow the sun will die.

A quiet spectacular,
        accompanied by dead soldiers,

and women dying in childbirth.
A vulture lights up the earth.

The warrior's chin
                moves the serpent's tongue.

See, the veils of blue lift, the flesh
streams off.   Then there is bone.

Nothing else but a roar between the legs.

The skeleton of the world appears singing.

KAFKA'S DIARY

The world is conquered and we have watched it with open eyes.
We can therefore quietly turn away and live on.

—*Diary*, Franz Kafka

Gales blow flower into warrior.
The armada's great white
petals float olive seas.

O Ancestor,

live mask of hammered gold,

do you see the children's throats cry open
with your hollow eyes of storm?

Wicker cages shake with parrot screams,
stone ways run with blood and spice, spilled.

A machete sings to a leashed neck.

All the plumage of a heritage lost.

There are no pictures. How would a family look?
The homeless child plays

all the sounds of father and mother.

Spell of dirt calling to water,
press ghostly lips to clavicle,
cloak us all in a long embrace.

OF RED & WHITE CLOVER

Of his dark skin, of her fair skin,
of his braided black hair, of her
perfume, of petal, fur, stamen,
foxglove, hydrangea, of his
saguaro, of her coral azalea,
of his gaunt fingers and long
torso, of apple fall, of iris, of his
vagabond, of her debutante,
of her blonde, of golden chain
bloom, of avocado tree, of lime,
of his Spanish twang, of his red
chile ristras, of his disappearance,
of her blue grey eyes, of her fast
driving and slow gardening, of her
softball pitching arm, of his
guitar, her petite waist, of her
roast chicken, of my olive skin,
my dark hooded eyes, I arrive
full of unasked questions,
of his mystery, of their pride,
of my shyness, my retreat to tulip
and hickory thick forests, please
do not ask me who I am or where
I'm from, I'm gone to the woods
with snake plant and rain owlet.

DAUGHTER POEM GOING NOWHERE

Nature does what is difficult. But someone is always anxious.
Do birds think about building nests when it's not spring?
How are you mastering your darkness? In the bright
Los Angeles light who remembers a father walking these streets
to his end under lanky palms and pawn shops.
The man and the woman are gone. But to be a daughter
is forever. There, touch the sweet part of my arm where it bends.
Quick, before perfection sets its blinding sun.
Tell me again how he always kept a bunch of carrots in his pocket.

CANTE MADRE, MOTHER SONG

He sent her the whip
so she'd know it was
time to come back.

He sent her the black
braid that once ran
black down his back.

She sent him the dotted
scarf, red silk wrapped
with a knife inside.

Papa the lover,
Papa the loner.
Mama you're gone,
Mama you're song.

ANCIENT SONG OF THE EDIBLE FLOWER

Mouth has planted
a garden filled with its own death
Acrobatic, her thoughts
are spits, are sacrifice.
And teeth and tongue are song.

Mouth is fertile,
her words are long
pollens of squash blossom.

In spring mouth's cavern fills
with bats who come for the white cactus
flower of la pitahaya de la noche.

In summer mouth fills with dragon fruit.

The place was only birds when the Aztecs came,

they made it run with water   and the water fills with stars

and the occasional bloodletting.

Then the soldiers landed and killed and stayed,
and horses owned the roads.

What is the word for what we keep forgetting?

Reverse echo,
the word is sand, *la arena.*
La arena de la playa.

It is sand,   tiniest glass world   of waves crashing.

CANTE BRUJA, WITCH SONG

Mija, learn sorrow before learning to speak.
Ashy-faced bird, sharpen your spear

      to draw the pattern of sad, the pattern of joy
      when you look at what you are made of.

I don't see my face, owl says before soaring,
as the future is born of slave and colonizer
            on the ledge of the window.

Pequeña, your flamenco
          mother dances for the sea now.
She left windmills to sail from Spain to Mexico.
Dancing *siguiriyas* under the waves.

     You are now an orphan. *La bruja* will sing
the story while you pick tobacco leaves in Mazatlán.

Father will change his name each year until he vanishes.

CANTE TORTILLA

Red bowl shallow and wide, color of innards,
clay the texture of fingers pressing to get out.

Dish moving with what it once held,
skin crawling to find a body.

Sadness possessed,
quiero mi dolor.

Nana, teach me to make tortillas.
Mix with hands, add two scoops fat.

In the mango-painted kitchen slapping dough.
Knead and squeeze in fist. Flour, water, crisis.

Rest four minutes in a towel-covered bowl,
maybe your long lost son will come home.

Press dough on hot skillet.
Shape me in sorrow, I will spread like a sun.

BIRD SCULPTURE AS WHISTLE & FATHER

Once enchanted,
I did not forget your voice,
me encanta el sonido de tu voz.
I took it from its dark sheath
to drag the twang by the metal
strings waiting in shame and fear
of its raw song.
Father, you are an angel painting
feathers on the wings of a young angel.
These legs are not mine,
they dance me.
This flesh is not mine,
it swims in the brine of heaven.

YUCATÁN

Mija, travel the day at night,
plant five fields for the maize god,

      wear a braided pelt of corn husk.

Drink chocolate, crawl to power.
      Sink into the watery world.

      Shield drawn by a little girl

in Cozumel, land of turkeys,
      deer and caravels of soldiers.

      Protect me from my own myth.

A voice swallows the island
      and speaks from the tower.

La Voz says *Mija,* you look like your father only lighter.

We called him *Prieto,* the dark one.

PRIETO, PRIETA

The thing inside the
thing inside the thing
inside Malinche,
mother, Cortés, father,
casta, first *mestizo*,
loanword for admixture,
dark one, darker than
one and lighter than
the other, *espaldera*,
graft, hybrid, *pardo*, *parda*,
castiza, like the heads
inside the heads inside
the heads of sculptures
of gods, men, frogs,
jaguar, serpent, mixed
one of lavish lineage.

AZTEC CLOWN SINGING

Great jaguar paw holding the dead,
your world will come to an end.

In my underground volcanic
I am fan and rattles. Stealing

cochineal from the cacti, I'm thief
of sixty shades of blood, mashing

bright beetles with mortar and pestle.
I paint the warrior and quainter objects.

I rub the city carmine. The longer
I grind the more precious the red.

VOICE AS SCULPTURE

The heart beating inside the bowl says—
what is underground we keep safer.
What is above is not to be trusted,
it dies, burns, flies away, gets pummeled,
abducted, hidden below deck, vanished by waves.
The flayed one, sacrificed for spring planting, says—
then put my blood in the whelk spoon carved
as a human hand and carry it to the sea.

FÁBULA

...y el sol dentro de la tarde,
como el hueso en una fruta.

La panocha guarda intacta,
su risa amarillo y dura.

Fábula, Federico García Lorca

Houses owned by the supernatural, forests of mountains
before the drop to sea. Live chickens on their way
to market on the long night bus ride across Mexico.
Men with machine guns stop us at checkpoints to nudge
crates of candy and calabash. I'm here to see where
I come from to stop the din of not knowing. Mazatlán,
Yucatán, Ibiza, Alsace. Indigo streets of San Juan,
vineyards of the Rhineland. Dirt floor in Phoenix. Tobacco
barn in New England. Coffin maker, crucifix carver,
furniture builder, tobacco picker, fruit grower, goldpanner,
wallpaperer. Did they sing?

ICQUINYAOCALTZACCA

In Nahuatl the word means
shut into the palace with war.

Fighting scarlet horsemen.
Within the plumed soldiers,

wet red tanks beating, waiting to fire.
Without a face. Without a blood.

A detailed account would be endless.
We have been delirious,

been desired, been battered.
Of ships crossing the horizon,

who invited you? Tell me, asks the skin
of one who lies on the beach watching.

Tell me, flower moving across water.
Will you be gentle or harsh against me?

Suitcase of uncertainty.
Like conquistador.

Doors closed on all sides. No one gets out.
Then more warriors surround the city.

Like moat. Like wall. Ever separate.
Symmetrical and always evening.

DESTINY RELOCATED

While I sleep someone
paves the river, darkest
therianthropy, beyond
the work of werewolf,
skin-walker and trickster,
mercuric line
rushing with traffic
apocalypse over
what once flowered.
Mouth, a veil of sighs.
Her throat, a trauma
that if it could be told
would be a history
of truth moving as
fever through night,
charging the horizon
like horses shipboard,
neighing lost to
the sound of waves,
then from salt to battle.

VIOLET

PRIMERO SUEÑO, FIRST DREAM:
ON CROSSING, A WHITMANESQUE

What is it then between us?

¿Qué es entonces entre nosotros?

My horse is afraid of you and both of us are thirsty.

Stone face, we crossed the seas from Spain,

I've been riding for days past pyramids in Mexico.

Whatever it is, it avails not—distance avails not,

and place avails not. My horse and I are tired

of the blistering desert. Who is your family,

crowd of great heads in a field?

Who has conquered you and whom will I now conquer?

Big rock, your lips look like ancient waves.

Your mouth reminds me of my wife's kisses goodbye.

I am lonely as the moon. *Por favor,* speak to me,

face in the grass. I remember the first time

I put my fingers inside a woman, and the first time

she put her fingers inside herself.

I too had receiv'd identity by my body,

my body the body uncertain, my body mixed,

dreaming of being a Spanish conquistador,

dreaming of being an Olmec head, carved and mouth sealed

forever. *Keep your places, objects than which none else*

is more lasting. We plant you permanently within us.

Being what—an across, a Zarathustra, a span

of scarf woven of seventeen colors from what roams,

what flies, what swims and what sings.

Being a woman and a man, stone-crafted and aqueous,

being brown, being tree and flood-tide,

being free citizen of the body earth, electing in revolt

to expand and bring down whatever rises between us.

STICHOMYTHIA, A STUDIO VISIT

DIEGO VELÁZQUEZ: What if I put myself in all the portraits with
horses

FRIDA KAHLO: And you put monkeys on horses

VELÁZQUEZ: Suppose I visit your land of pyramids and tombs

KAHLO: Then the paintings on the wall of *Las Meninas*
would be of Aztec warriors

VELÁZQUEZ: The painting I am painting in *Las Meninas*
is of you

KAHLO: Suppose the Indians visit Spain first, putting kayaks
in at Cadaqués

VELÁZQUEZ: Dalí makes lunch for you all at his villa

KAHLO: Surrealism caused by colonialism

VELÁZQUEZ: Suppose the urge to paint is the same as the urge to
conquer

KAHLO: The urge for war is a miscarriage of man

VELÁZQUEZ: It is the urge to pray

KAHLO: It is the urge to prey

VELÁZQUEZ: *Autorretrato*

KAHLO: *Auto-da-fé*

LA MENINA

Yes, it's a great painting and then you look
at all the lace that needs starching like empire.

Men who fell in love with the effects of hell.
Here's the cross, here is perishing.

You were free and then someone came to your shore
and you were not. She was dragged from her mother.

The soldier cut off her hands, he stabbed
her first. Imagine how 800 towns burned

in the kingdom of Jalisco. I'd rather think about
the dog in the painting. He faces us, his paws

reaching out. We can't see his eyes but we know
he's a good dog, a loyal, gentle mutt.

QUERIDA

Lima beans and cherries.

Spain in summer sustenance.

From Mexico, Fray Diego Durán writes,
In famine a handful of beans is like plucking off eyelashes.

The festival of the hand. Cut off. Harvested.

Embryonic shimmer.

Quiero, quiero, quiero.

THEATER OF WAR

GLINDA THE GOOD WITCH:
    You flew your broomstick to Madrid?

BRUJA DOROTHY:
    I saved Goya's Black Paintings for last.
    But after Rubens's Saturn, Goya was cartoonish.
    Rubens paints an old man eating his son,
    it's terribly human, he takes the myth literally.
    Goya paints a parody of prowess, age coveting youth.

GLINDA THE GOOD WITCH:
    Dear, dear, dear.

BRUJA DOROTHY:
    Not just myths and *brujas*—
    what struck me were the piles of bodies.

GLINDA THE GOOD WITCH:
    Dear, dear, dear,
    like the house that crushed my sister.

BRUJA DOROTHY:
    The paintings speak to me,
    say we keep cutting, butchering, slaying.
    We have too much language for destruction,
    we can't stop, words spill into our hands to make us do it.

GLINDA THE GOOD WITCH:
    We forget there are words
    with the habit of surrender,
    words like tenderly and cherish.

BRUJA DOROTHY:
>They moved Goya's frescos from his house to the Prado.
>Other hands touching his brushstrokes.
>It bothers me.

GLINDA THE GOOD WITCH:
>Witchcraft atop witchcraft. Surrender, Dorothy.

LETTER FROM THE BRUJA TO CORTÉS

When the earth cancels herself

with new skin flayed from the old,
     recall the symmetry of bones.

You know the priest is hiding in the tower
speaking prophecy in the voice of a god.

Try on the shirt of coyote first,

          then the bird suit of yellow flight.
Try on the armor of terrapin.

Inside the victim's mouth
  hunt for parched fangs of the rain god.

               Under crocodile stars
blow the trumpet for the slain deer.

          Only then, when you touch the vessel
with its procession of warriors,

          will you traverse a flaw in the world
          to emerge with the head of a lynx.

               I step through the sea's door
with green staining my hand,

          still no one answers my questions.

Tell me why someone must always be
sacrificed for the future to be assured?

MYTHIC ENCOUNTER

Evolution enters wearing a feathered cape:

Where's my parrot? Hand me my arrows,
somebody get these monkeys out of the way,
we have a visitor. Who goes there?

Cortés, on horseback, says: I am come from Spain by armada.
Is this the Gold Place? I have a thirst.

Evolution, not on horseback, says: You will need to keep going, there's
little for you here.

CORTÉS: But what of all the noise?

EVOLUTION: The sound of birds before killing.

CORTÉS: And where lives the leader of the Seven Cities of Gold?

EVOLUTION: I drank his blood in an hourglass.

CORTÉS: And where is your god?

EVOLUTION: I drank his blood in an hourglass.

DIARIO

From the letters of Hernán Cortés to Charles V,
translated by Anthony Pagden

The figures of the idols
are much larger than the body
of a big man. They are made of dough
from all the seeds and vegetables
which they eat, ground and mixed
together, and bound with the blood
of human hearts which those priests
tear out while still beating.

        Since finding this tin
        I have been making daily,
        and continue to make,
        a few guns; so far five
        pieces have been completed.

When I saw how determined
they were to die in their defense
I burnt and tore down the towers
of their idols and their houses.

        After it had pleased Our Lord God
        I ordered that those who were taken
        alive should be branded
        with your Highness's mark.

We burned the houses
and then the tiny houses
of the birds of every species.
When we saw how much
it hurt them we burned them all.

HISTORY OF SHIELDS

Arrow, how many times you flew

from the naming of shields.

Shield of Moctezuma, bird-snake of light,

Aztec of feathers, arrow of a dare,

of being barely there and gone,

shield of jungle blue flight,

of what once flew beyond touch of spear.

Esoteric aortic object spinning.

Hero asleep at the wheel of good,

how to understand a shield for consequence?

Shield of Achilles hovering endlessly,

what possible action, of what vast darkness,

shield of fear. Leonardo's shield of lizard,

of snake, form from the dark pond of mind.

Wrap the heart in the box of what crawls

to see what comes out.

Arrow, your mind's mad camera chases

victim. Shield on shield on shield apotropaic,

keep us safe from evil. Shield of conscience,

hold the world away.

LADY OF THE DRY BRANCHES

A Voice tells me to slip
the painting at Madrid's National Museum
into my purse.
Our Lady of the Snow goes with me now,

I know what she is thinking.

As it snows on each twig
golden prayers on the branches
hang heavy with frost flowers.
Each letter is an *Ave Maria.*

The word is a moon glint.

In perpetual night a Voice says
I've snowflakes in my eyes.
I'm thermal.
All the birds are white now,
whole flocks of them.

Swans swaying in formations
of ribbon tying and untying
the brightness of the cold world.

Someone drops an ermine cloak
about the babe and me.

MADONNA OF EL MUSEO DE AMÉRICA

In Madrid no one else is visiting the museum of what
the conquerors took from America. Surrounding
it are fields of blood poppies, umbrella trees, blonding
grass, a little shrine for the Virgin. *Tell her your troubles,*
a sign says, *here is paper to write on, tie it to the gate*
with a wish. Inside the museum percolate hundreds of heads.
Shelves of eyes and feathers. A harvest face with ears of corn,
a face for rain, a face for sickness, a face in pain
with doors that open to another face inside for faith.

THE BOY'S FACE IN TOLEDO

Tenderly he lowers the dead man
to his coffin. Boy angelic trusting the body
to an actual angel who raises him through
a dilation in clouds. El Greco paints hands
on the church wall with marvelously long
slender fingers, and faces with wide eyes
awakened from the dream of resembling
nothing any mortal has ever seen.

TOLL

A hollow knock more
than a ring. Sound of
being wanted. In childhood
they rang the cowbell's lung
to call me from the woods.
Uxmal's sun follows the old
fisherman who has buried all
his children with strong arms
of sea. He circles the church
to tug the bell ropes to ring
one of the choices to be
human. Under his orange
yellow city sleep pyramids
from his ancestors enticing
gods of weather to fabricate
astonishing bridges from
desolation to desolation.

SUBTRACTION TREE

A fable. A tree

so big all the town's children
hold hands around it.

The invaders are coming,
we are too few to meet them.

We hide the town under the Tule tree.

Everyone is happy living under it
so we stay forever.

A boy points out monkeys and iguanas
in knots with a flashlight.

Under the tree
I dream I am one of three warriors

waiting to meet the army,
I hear the sound of hooves.

Montezuma cypress,
2,000 years old, what have you seen?

In time of drought nuns from the church
bring you their precious drinking water.

The tree is getting bigger.

CANTE ROTO, BROKEN DOWN SINGING

So many words for broken—
quebrado, fracturado, interrumpido,
deshecho, violado, arruinado, destrozado,
chapurreado, abatido, cascado.
Each one a beginning.

ADORED

*...there came toward us four Indian chieftains with a flag of gold,
which weighed some four gold marks, on a pole, and by this they gave
us to understand that they came in peace...*
                          —Hernán Cortés, *The Third Letter*

Kings sending slaves into rock face,
conquistadors launching murders of gleaming

armadas. From the earth, metal—to the mask,
metal, across seas to Spanish altars.

Durer writes of seeing a six-foot orb of gold
carried from the new land.

Golden husk of empire melted for a prayer.
History's gilded mirror is a long blinding

stare. My family in California panning creeks
with tin plates, finding broken bits of bowls

mixed in the earth with roots. Pieces of the old
story of the heart shrapnelled

like the Mimbres burial of a woman. On her head
she wears a dish killed with a hole broke in it

so the painted turtle can circle her skull
as her soul rises up through the earth's maw.

LATINA STARBOX

Always brilliance beside barbarism—

                              vast pools at Teotihuacán
                              filling with stars at night.

Speculation: It was never about the gold,
just a curiosity for what lies around

                         the bend. Man Emerging from
Seashell. Woman with Bundle on Her Head.

Stone Object of Unknown Use.
Terracotta Life-Size Figure of Skeleton.

                         Young Deer Toy on Wheels.
                         Sculpture Resembling a Stirrup.

Fat clay dogs feed the dead in the afterworld. Food leads
the body toward its future.

Evolution is only one answer—

                         found in a cave wearing the flayed
skin of a victim.   Evolution is optimistic.

It is blood flower electric.
                It is mouths in a red pile echoing.

Me is still a dream at night,
                  El tecolote's wings plunge into my air.

Darktime, I say to him.

                               Darktime, he says back.

FIRE-TAKING

Aztec girl twisting her hair into a braid when the army arrives.

>   She sees them in her citadel,
>   her nickname for the city
>   forgotten by her mouth's mind.

The Spanish writer who keeps the oldest codex saw grief
when the people's prayers were burned by the soldiers.

Havoc, my freedom, without a history I invent my own.

>   Say I am of many faces,
>   neither white nor brown,
>   say violet,
>   the color that speaks like violence.

Legacy sounds like lost at sea.

>   Say it wasn't precious to me, identity.
>   Strange, dangerous innocence.

Earth is an onion strung with lights, my eyes sting from the blaze.

A gold hawk joins
            the ring of fox in heavy dew around me early and I
            am part of their wet ritual in my wish

                    to turn from what is human,

even knowing it was hawk who stole woodpecker's redheaded flight.

SCI-FI CANTE

The sun blows down.
Under cover of night we move bags of earth.
Where we go will be far, dark, cold.
Light years later we disembark
to another place, another chance,
pressing handfuls of dirt to our mouths.
The same soil we once walked
and never knew we loved.

POSSESSED

Mother and father, both in my hands

speaking as I hold
the brush to paint.

What's that thing when forms repeat
across generations?   No, not stolen fire.

The jungle, how it grows,

especially vines
advancing like soldiers.

This summer, climbing
buckwheat scrawling itself
across bee balm and goldenrod fields.

I want it to be you, mother,
covering me everywhere

but I am pulling its red thread off the gold
so bees can feed.

When the bobcat visits
she is my mother and not the vine,
my chest rejoices.

She is mother and father
telling me to keep painting the sun.

Wheels of flame

warming hands in the grave.

HUNGRY SINGING, CANTE HAMBRIENTO

Melt me
down
into a spoon
or knife
in silver
service to
your mouth
amor
all the Spanish
verbs to pray
orar
rezar
rogar
suplicar
rezábamos
para que
saliera el sol
querido
let us care
for the earth
pray only
for the moon
to rise

ACKNOWLEDGMENTS

I am thankful for many inspiring words over years of reading and research, including Anthony Pagden's *Hernán Cortés: Letters from Mexico*; Herma Briffault's translation of Bartolomé de las Casas's *The Devastation of the Indies*; *Maya Cosmos* by David Freidel, Linda Schele and Joy Parker; Dennis Tedlock's *Popol Vuh*; Doris Heyden's translation of Fray Diego Durán's *The History of the Indies of New Spain*; *Mexico South: The Isthmus of Tehuantepec* by Miguel Covarrubias; and the poetry and prose of Sor Juana Inés de la Cruz, Octavio Paz and Federico García Lorca. Also, I am grateful for a Poets House fellowship and the Lower Manhattan Cultural Council Workspace Residency where this book began. Thank you to my wonderful, supportive circle of family and friends. Gratitude to Elizabeth Zuba. Michel Franck, thanks for joining me on the raft.

Thank you to the editors of the following journals in which these poems first appeared:

Boston Review: "Trading Post" and "Diary of the Ghost of a Mestiza."

Battery Journal: "Possessed" and "Madonna of El Museo de América."

Brooklyn Poets Chapbook, *What is it then between us? Celebrating 200 Years of Walt Whitman*, edited by Jason Koo. Whitman bicentennial poetry contest (selected by Mark Doty): "Primero Sueño, First Dream: On Crossing, A Whitmanesque."

FENCE: "Dear Conquistador, We Already Invented the Wheel," "Portrait of a Spanish Mexican Maid," and "Stichomythia: A Studio Visit."

La Presa: "Bird Sculpture as Whistle & Father," "Cante Tortilla," "Of Red & White Clover," "Indigo, Indigoing, Indigone," "Icquinyaocaltzacca," "Cante Bruja, Witch Song," and "Yucatán."

Massachusetts Review: "Curiosity Has More Syllables Than Conquer."

MIT Press, *What Nature Anthology*: "Diary of the Ghost of a Mestiza."

Poetry Magazine: "Afterword," "Call & Response Between Colonizer & Colonized," "Prieto, Prieta," "Un Tintero, Inkwell," and "Fire-Taking."

Schuylkill Valley Journal, Whitman folio: "Primero Sueño, First Dream: On Crossing, A Whitmanesque."

University of Oklahoma Press, *Other Musics: Anthology of Latina Poets*, edited by Cynthia Cruz, 2019: "Small Model of Mexican Ruin."

Desirée Alvarez is a poet and painter whose first book, *Devil's Paintbrush*, won the 2015 May Sarton New Hampshire Poetry Award. Her poetry is anthologized in *What Nature* (MIT Press), *Other Musics: New Latina Poetry* (University of Oklahoma Press), and published in *Boston Review*, *FENCE*, and *Poetry*. Awarded the Glenna Luschei Poetry Award, fellowships from NYFA and Poets House, she exhibits widely as a visual artist and was awarded by the American Academy of Arts and Letters. Alvarez graduated from Wesleyan University and School of Visual Arts. She teaches at CUNY and The Juilliard School.

Raft of Flame
By Desirée Alvarez

Cover art:
Peacable Kingdom by Desirée Alvarez,
2007, ink on fabric, installation detail. www.desireealvarez.com.

Cover typeface: Kabel LT Std and Cronos Pro
Interior typeface: Adobe Garmond Pro and Cronos Pro

Cover & interior design by Trisha Peck

Printed in the United States
by Books International, Dulles, Virginia
On 55# Glatfelter B19 Antique
Acid Free Archival Quality Recycled Paper

Publication of this book was made possible in part by gifts from
Katherine & John Gravendyk in honor of Hillary Gravendyk,
Francesca Bell, Mary Mackey, and The New Place Fund

Omnidawn Publishing
Oakland, California
Staff and Volunteers, Spring 2020

Rusty Morrison & Ken Keegan, senior editors & co-publishers
Kayla Ellenbecker, production editor
Gillian Olivia Blythe Hamel, senior editor & book designer
Trisha Peck, senior editor & book designer
Rob Hendricks, marketing assistant & *Omniverse* editor
Cassandra Smith, poetry editor & book designer
Sharon Zetter, poetry editor & book designer
Liza Flum, poetry editor
Matthew Bowie, poetry editor
Juliana Paslay, fiction editor
Gail Aronson, fiction editor
Izabella Santana, fiction editor & marketing assistant
SD Sumner, copyeditor